CONFIDENT IS *She*

A QUEEN'S GUIDE TO RECLAIMING HER THRONE AND REIGNING WITH CONVICTION

STORIES COMPILED BY

LATOYA GARRETT

Dedication

To every woman who has been disappointed, rejected, abused, manipulated and misused.

You deserve God's best.

Table of Contents

Introduction

When you go for a drive, what seat do you sit in? Driver's seat, back seat, or passenger seat? If it's any other seat than the driver's seat, you are in the wrong seat and going absolutely nowhere. Driving a car requires you to be behind the wheel to steer it in the direction it should go. Your foot should be on the accelerator to increase speed or maintain speed, and your foot should be prepared to engage the break when you need to slow down or stop. You can't do any of those actions if you are not in your rightful position.

The only way to take your rightful position is by leaving the back seat. Your Queendom can only be steered in the direction it should go when you are in the driver's seat. You are *required* to drive because backseat driving is NOT possible. How annoying it is for someone in the back seat to tell the driver how to drive! Also imagine how unrealistic and illogical it is to tell the empty driver's seat how to drive.

Taking the back seat is sometimes the most appealing choice for the weary, the disappointed, the hurt, and the rejected. I get it. When life seems to be getting the best of me, I want to hide from all my responsibilities because I can evade pain and discomfort. I believe you have felt the same way, which caused you to make a choice. A choice keeping you in the same monotonous cycle.

You took the backseat willingly.

But to tell the truth, there's a restless, anxious feeling invading your spirit now. The mediocrity you settled for is no longer comfortable. Deep in the recesses of your heart, you want more. The space you're in is choking you, and you know why. God set an expiration date for where you are. The time has come for you to stop hiding. Get in the driver's seat and let God navigate you to where He wants you to go.

How do you reclaim the driver's seat? Do the work. Make up your mind to claw, crawl and whatever else is necessary to reclaim your position. Know that God is there. Remind yourself that He's been there for you before, and He's waiting for you to get on board with Him again.

I was in the back seat at one point as well, grieving the disappointments of life until I grasped the divine understanding God had already put before me to pull myself out of the pit of repetitive living. Every day seemed to be crowded with the same purposeless feeling. All color had faded, and I went through the motions. Then, the day came when I got fed up. My resurgence happened when I did the work. I prayed, took webinars, studied, read, and learned to uncover hidden grievances in my heart. I aired my frustrations about God, myself and situations to God. At the end of those conversations, I told God I trusted Him. My process took me down avenues of knowledge where I faltered but planted seeds to push me to where I am now, though I am still a work in progress.

One thing I've learned on this faith journey is that I am royalty. I am a QUEEN who has *thee* say-so in her Queendom. My realignment with God gave me the unshakeable confidence that I am His, and He gave me the wonderful task of helping the next woman regain her confidence as well.

And this book, *Confident Is She*, is about getting you, the Queen, back on your throne to reign with conviction. As you read the personal testimonies and complementing faith-suggestive chapters that precede or follow, make the choice to fight for your future.

Your Queendom has been missing its Queen.

Has your excuse been the story you've rehearsed and told yourself? The "It hurts too much, so I deserve to rest and grieve" story. Your characterization of resting and grieving has turned into multiple years of immobility. Now, you are stuck. Nah, you owe it to yourself to get unstuck. The story you tell yourself has to change.

No one is coming to save you...again. Jesus already did that. You've been waiting for someone to rule on your behalf, but the someone you've been looking for is YOU! Your life is not a Tesla where it can self-drive itself. No ma'am! Your life requires intentional input from you. Put your hands on the wheel, release the break, shift into drive and accelerate. Time to put your hands to work again. Your life will regain its purposeful vitality as God directs you to the destination you should've been all along.

While you were in the back seat, you allowed your mind to be reprogrammed to believe that comfortability and stagnation is as good as it's going to get. That's a lie from the enemy. Take a leap of faith. The effort may seem hard and uncomfortable, but you have to rebuild those spiritual muscles (muscle memory). During the rebuilding phase, God will impart and provide, and before you know it, you'll have reclaimed your throne in totality. Because confidence in God generates confidence in self.

Queen let's get you back on your throne.

Stately Inquiry

Remember the days when you were so full of ideas, hopes and dreams. Remember how you executed your plans without the fear of failure. Remember how overwhelmingly amazing it was to achieve your goals. Remember how it felt to be genuinely happy and at peace, living purposefully. Do you remember?

Now tell me, why don't you dream anymore? Why haven't you attempted to implement at least one of your ideas? Why don't you hope for the best? Why is fear of failure the first thing that dissuades you whenever you do get an idea? Why aren't you trying anymore? Why have you settled for monotony and soundless chaos?

You no longer have to wear insecurity as a protective cloak. What you do have to do is get to the root of your lack of confidence. Know the causation so you can grasp the solution. Consider when you lost your confidence, what caused you to lose it, who were all involved, and how life changed for you after. Let the memories flow.

One or several things contributed to your confidence deficit. Abuse, assault, divorce, weight gain, unmet expectations, illness, financial loss, loss of freedom, death, drug abuse, life-changing accident etc. Something happened to you, and you allowed it to define you. However, the opportunity to establish a new interpretation of the woman you are and the opportunity to authentically live again is your choice.

Do you prefer to continue to live like a peasant or do you prefer the alternative to live in splendor? Choose the latter and change your life. New life begins when you decide.

Chapter 1

Your Queendom, Your Responsibility

Crowned

Your Queendom is solely your responsibility. Pawning your responsibility off on someone else or letting it lag behind is a no-no. What is a Queendom? I'm glad you asked. A Queendom is your life, your purpose, your health. The people and things connected to you are a part of your Queendom. Everything about you-past, present, and future-makes up your Queendom. So, it's imperative that you know who you are and whose you are. Because not knowing means the enemy has prevailed in making you forget your true identity.

Knowing who you are and whose you are will reveal how healthy your Queendom truly is. Let's face it, questioning your identity signifies you are not in optimal health. You are obligated in finding out just who you are outside of the "mommy, wife, daughter, sister, bestie" roles. Ask yourself: When I'm not playing my role(s), who am I? Am

I reacting to situations and/or people the same way I have been because that's how I was trained to react? Do I like how I react to them? Am I stimulated or repressed in my reaction? Have I allowed myself to entertain things and people that are not conducive to my growth? Am I allowing life to happen without my conscious input?

Still a little fuzzy about how to answer those questions? That's okay. The number one and surefire way to get clarity and understanding of who you are is by knowing whose you are. You belong to God. A relationship with Him answers all those questions and exculpates the fog keeping you from knowing Him and yourself. First and foremost, when you know God, you begin to know yourself. Get to know God by spending time with Him and His word.

There are life-affirming scriptures in God's word, and they emphasize the identity of the believer. God made you and gave you life (Job 33:4). Not only were you "made" by God, but He also knit you together with precision and intentionality, creating the most wonderful work of art (Psalm 139:13-14). If you value something your hands toiled to create, you keep it under your protection (Psalm

17:8). God ultimately displayed His love for you, for us by giving us the offer of reconciliation that spans until Jesus' return (John 3:16). He is saying that you and I are worth it. Accepting God's offer of reconciliation means you now belong to Him and have become a new person (2 Corinthians 5:17 & John 1:12). One of my personal affirming scriptures comes from 1 Peter 2:9 which says, *"But you are not like that, for you are a chosen people. You are royal priests, a holy nation, God's very own possession. As a result, you can show others the goodness of God, for he called you out of the darkness into his wonderful light."*

1 Peter 2:9 in its entirety verifies your identity. To know you were chosen, selected, handpicked and seen as special is shout worthy. A mistake? No ma'am, you are not. The scripture goes on to say that "you are royal priests." Gotta unpack that, right? Royal is defined as having the status of a king or queen or a member of their family. There's the indisputable evidence. Honey, you are a Queen. And your duty as a royal entity and a chosen vessel of God is to proclaim God's praises to whomever and wherever. This is a universal and a personal purpose. First proclaim God's praises to yourself and your Queendom so you can

proclaim His praises to the masses. Gotta have some experience in what you are teaching. The rest of verse nine is about the continuous development of your connection to God, foretelling your testimony. And people are thirsty to hear and gain inspiration from a person with direct experience in shirking despair and embracing wholeness.

This is why your identity is detrimental to your Queendom. It's not just about you but about others as well. The ones who will follow your lead (i.e., your family, employees etc.) need you to be in the proper alignment. Falling for the enemy's tactics of confusion makes you question your existence and thus causes misalignment. Don't fall for the okey doke.

Be intentional in your pursuit in your relationship with God. Seeking Him above all else will add everything else you need. Yes, you still have to do the work. You will never *not* have to do your part. Be healthy in mind, body and spirit. Girl, get you some rest! Rest is essential in maintaining your health all around. Learn yourself. What brings you joy? What pastimes do you desire to indulge in? Get to know you! This is your responsibility. The decision alone is yours.

I read recently in one of my morning devotionals authored by Rick Warren where he said that we choose how much God blesses us. I was like *huh...how?* I mean God is God, and He chooses whether or not and to bless and when to bless. Right? Yes, He does, but you also have authority as well. The decisions you make, the consistency and discipline you apply, your humility and faith determine how God blesses you. Faith and works provide the provision.

Keep in mind that this is a process and a lifelong journey because as you grow, you continue to evolve. Tastes change. Goals change. Bodies change. Nothing stays the same. So, as the season changes, you will too, and you'll continue to learn more about yourself as time goes on.

Your Queendom needs you back at the helm. The vacancy sign has been sitting there long enough. Stop self-sabotaging and stop making excuses and know it's **<u>not</u>** too late. No matter what you've done, God is waiting for you to get back to Him so He can show you how to govern what He's blessed you with.

Dethrone the lies, the pain and the past disappointments. Straighten up your crown and sit upon your throne.

Here are some tips on how to start this process:
1. Submit to God (humility)
2. Pray consistently (building relationship)
3. Read & Study the Word (learning God & self)
4. Listen to God's voice (faith)
5. Be obedient to God's instructions (works)

While you're following these tips, you'll be learning about yourself. Take the time to take care of you so you can properly take care of your Queendom. How does taking care of yourself look to you? Do some research if you are not versed in self-care. Take full inventory of your environment. Reduce or eliminate the negligible and increase the essentials. What doesn't serve or nurtures growth in the Queendom must go.

Time to go to work, Queen. You are more than a conqueror.

Chapter 2

Beauty Redefined

By **Latoya Garrett**

Never would I have thought the majority of my thirty plus years of life would've been gripped by a personal burden, illusioned so large and imposing prior, now seems so insignificant. Insignificant in terms of emotional importance and social dependency. And if I could go back and tap five-year-old me on the shoulder, I would tell the happy, imaginative burgeoning me that my beauty is subjective to others but unique to self.

For as long as I can remember, the number five has always been my favorite number, and once I found out it's biblical significance, I was endeared to the number even more. Number five symbolizes God's grace, and I can't help but think after the long journey of doubting myself that the number five being my favorite number is God's way of subliminally telling me He graced me to endure what I did.

It happened in 1990. The day the seed was planted which caused me to doubt me for over thirty years. Don't know the day of the week or month, but I'm sure of the year, and I'm sure of the identity of the man who spewed jealous contempt he held towards me. Crazy thing is, this memory didn't resurface until the spring of 2020 when I asked God to reveal the root of the emotional fluctuation I was experiencing more frequently. I'd been doing the internal work to break free from the old mindset of feeling inferior based on my outward appearance, however I was still struggling. Yes, this memory was a repressed memory I believe the enemy orchestrated. According to psychological experts, repressed memories occur when something traumatic happens. Not in my case. The enemy came at me in a way that people wouldn't declare the situation as a traumatic event. However, he came at me when I was most vulnerable to emotional manipulation and planted seeds of doubt and insecurity that blossomed into emotional disorder down the line. I was blinded to the events of that day in 1990 because my encounters with that "man" were brushed off by me as inconsequential. They were anything but inconsequential.

The "man" in question had died recently, and I remember telling my mother how I disliked him when I was a little girl. I didn't know why. I just knew I disliked him. My mother then told me how I had reason to dislike him. Her response surprised me because over the years, this man had become someone I cared about. She said he was always approaching me and talking to me crazy until her and my grandmother put a stop to it. After having the conversation with my mother, I went off to myself, and the memory of the root cause of my emotional fluctuation resurfaced.

While waiting for my mother to pick me up after school one day, this man, who I knew to be the father of one of my classmates, aggressively approached me while holding his daughter's hand. When I saw him, I immediately recoiled because he'd been confronting me on prior occasions, and for the life of me, I couldn't figure out why he was being so mean to me. That day he stomped up to me and said, "You think you pretty. You ain't pretty. My daughter looks better than you." I never responded because I didn't have to respond. I just remember my mother walking up and saying, "Didn't I tell you to stop messing with my baby?" She never knew what he'd said to me, only that he was standing over me. I never told her what he'd said, but I internalized it, along with every other thing he'd said to me during prior incidents. And everything he had said to me was based on my appearance.

The plethora of years after were engulfed in self-doubt and self-criticism. Every rejection and every disappointment was centered around the fact that I wasn't pretty enough. No matter what the situation was, I based what I perceived as "failure" on my outward appearance. My decisions, colored by a skewed self-belief, further exacerbated my insecurities. Though I couldn't remember how this mindset started, it had its grip on me so tight that I hid myself from others. I also camouflaged myself from myself so well that I was solely convinced that I had to adapt and stay in the background around certain people and conditions without bringing attention to myself in order to keep people from seeing the insecure person that I was. I clothed myself with this adaptive persona but grieved the real me. That grief manifested a shy, repressed person who always wanted more and developed an "I wish" fantasy mindset. Not only that, I used being mean as a shield to keep those, outside of my familial and small friendship circle, who truly wanted me for me away.

Social interactions during my school years did a number on my self-confidence as well. I couldn't chance being the target of my peers' jokes and mocking. I let opportunities pass me by because I was too scared to put myself out there for fear of the spotlight. I settled *a lot.* I wanted to be a cheerleader, but I settled for flag team. I wanted to be a leader of my class, but I stayed in the background. Then there were some instances when I couldn't escape the attention. Some of my peers wanted to know why I looked different from them, and some laughed because I may have been bigger than them. I was told I had man hands, looked flicted, was fat, my skin on my legs was weird, annoying etc. The false narrative I'd illogically built in my mind strengthened. Thinking I was concealing my inner emotional conflict, it actually oozed from my pores, and I drew the criticism I actually thought about myself. It compounded the contradicting feelings of not fitting in and my actions of trying to fit in that actually kept me socially inaccessible. I was in a psychological conundrum.

Away from school, witnessing the relationship between my parents also led to more insecurities as a young girl. The way my father treated my mother made me doubt any guy that had interest in me back then and moving forward. From my vantage point, cooking, cleaning, and taking care of the kids and home were all women were good for. Having a voice and defending self was a direct insult and not supported. Witnessing all of that made me question if my father could do it to my mother and it trickled down to me, how could any man do right by me? God showed me through my mother that although the situation wasn't ideal, someone verbally or physically accosting me had to be addressed. Although I hated conflict, I adopted the mindset that fighting back was necessary. However, I never adopted the mindset to address the emotional damage.

But something wonderful happened to me on a Tuesday night back in April 1999. I gave my life to God. Healing began that night. It took years for me to see the emotional damage I perpetuated on myself and allowed others to do as well. All through high school, there was this constant dichotomy of feelings fighting to reign supreme over my psyche. However, God had His hand on me, and slowly but surely, He revealed piece by piece how to regain my confidence.

I never had an accurate definitive name for the process at that time because I truly didn't comprehend what I was going through. I just knew I was tired of feeling inadequate, being ruled my own opinion and other's opinions on my outward appearance, and being a closet meanie to people unnecessarily. My distorted outlook was really the ugly I felt I looked like. My breakthrough came when something clicked on the inside of me one day, and I had a conversation with myself. I said, "Why do you care what others think? Their opinions don't matter. Every single negative thing you have thought about yourself manifested outwardly, but you can change the perception that you have about yourself." From that day, I intentionally forced myself to think positive about the physical features I believed were unattractive and told myself how I didn't have to accept being dismissed and overlooked by self and others.

This process has spanned years. It's still ongoing, and there are levels to this thing. And thank God I'm not where I used to be. God really protected me, and He didn't start working on me in 1999. God has been watching over me since the beginning. I could've been the type of girl who slept with any guy for validation. I didn't. I could've been the girl who fell for peer pressure. I refused to disappoint my mother. I could've been the girl who looked to other vices to feel good about myself. I couldn't add to what I was already going through. No, this process hasn't been easy nor without problems. There were times when I was in a rut, fighting against what God said about me. The conflict resulted in laziness and complacency. Weight gain happened. More criticism from people I engaged with about my faith and stance on waiting for marriage happened. Being told no man would ever wait for me happened. Not being able to find a job when I needed it most happened. Rejection and disappointment continued to happen. *More* weight gain happened. People initiating a conversation with me and then walking away when I opened my mouth to talk happened. Embracing introversion happened. While all of that was happening, God was still working.

I couldn't see God working, so sadness seeped in. Purpose was missing from my life, and I started to believe that maybe God didn't care about me. That old way of thinking revisited me, making me believe that even God didn't find me worthy of doing something of importance to advance His kingdom. Maybe I really was the ugly loser who didn't deserve to have good things happen to her. Anger added to the sadness, and I angrily accused God of not caring about me. Hadn't I suffered enough over the years emotionally? I desperately wanted to work for Him. Couldn't He see that? And if God didn't care, I knew people wouldn't either. The root cause of my mindset was still hidden, and though I had done some work to heal, I still hadn't quite grasped the concept of true beauty. God reminded me about John 3:16. He reminded me about being fearfully and wonderfully made in His image. He sent webinars I still don't know 'til this day how I came across them. The most unlikely people and connections happened that helped build up my faith in God and self. My purpose was revealed at this level of healing, and I now know I am purposed to lead, encourage and inspire through writing.

I became intentional about building myself up with the truth; God's word and my own personal convictions. Beauty is subjective, but it's unique to me. My true beauty doesn't lie in how I look on the outside. My true beauty radiates from my purpose in God and being His workmanship. Redefining beauty has freed me to embrace the real me. The quirky, nerdy and giggly me who loves what she loves without a care of who approves or not. I know I am beautiful, I am worthy, and I am God's own masterpiece. He's told me so, and I believe Him wholeheartedly. My past equipped me to walk in purpose for the sake of purpose.

Walking in this freedom and doing the intentional work still didn't absolve me from the more frequent highs and lows I started to experience the beginning of 2020. My spirit and my emotions were in a battle. The enemy didn't like this new level confidence, so he employed old tactics disguised differently. He had me questioning the strength of my faith. I still had faith, but I became negligent and allowed complacency to revisit. The root hadn't been exposed yet. This is why it's important to consistently maintain your deliverance, to keep you from falling back into old habits. I had enough faith to ask God to reveal what I couldn't see. And baby, the revelation floored me. It took a while for me to come to grips with those repressed memories, but another level of confidence transpired.

What I know is that the enemy tried to discredit what God had purposed for me to do at an early age. My standard of beauty was tied to my decisions and belief system. For so long, it worked until it didn't. I know the truth, and nothing can steer me away from it. Yes, I'm still a work in progress, but I shall not regress. I see myself as a confident woman of faith who will get even more bolder in the future. The pain of my past no longer has a hold on me. I challenge myself to do the uncomfortable, accept opportunities that scare me, and actively tell myself how beautiful I am. It's scary sometimes and uncomfortable, but it's also incredibly rewarding and exhilarating.

To the woman who struggles with her physical image, realize the origins of your struggle is internal. Surrender every lie and doubt to God and allow Him to heal your heart and infuse your spirit and emotions with His truth. Do the work, and embrace your new confidence. Intentionally and consistently believe you are beautiful because God doesn't make anything ugly.

Latoya Garrett, the Love & Faith author, resides in a small town in Louisiana. She's a 2007 graduate of Southeastern Louisiana University, where she obtained her Bachelor's degree in Psychology. Latoya is a full-time author of Black Christian Romance and Christian literature, owner and blogger of Inspiration by ToyaDenae, freelance editor and owner of Confident Queen Publishing. Latoya published her first book, *The Little Girl In You: Believe In Yourself*, in 2018 and has published and co-authored seventeen plus literary works (with more in the works).

Latoya is a huge advocate for women to be confident in their walk with God, in their faith, and everyday lives. Spreading confidence building encouragement through her own books of romance fiction, blog posts, and contributions to Christian literature is her God-given purpose. To accompany Confident Is She, she also released the journal, *Loving The Me I See*, to help women who struggle with their outward appearance.

Latoya knows one day that her prayers that one or more of her books being adapted into a feature film will become an answered prayer. She also aspires to write inspirational and thought-provoking screenplays for the big screen.

In her free time, Latoya is an avid reader who loves to discover new authors. She enjoys comedic television, action movies, The Walking Dead Universe, and the Marvel Universe. Her faith and family are top priorities. Gospel and 90s R&B are the music genres Latoya goes to for inspiration and nostalgia.

Check out her blog, author website, merch shop, & books at:
https://linktr.ee/toyadenae

Contact her: inspirationbytoyadenae@gmail.com

<u>Social Media</u>:

Facebook & Instagram- @authorlatoyagarrett

Twitter- @authorlatoyag

Chapter 3

Delivered But Moving The Same

State of Mind

Quick history lesson (or reminder lesson). An *exceptionally* long time ago, the children of Israel lived under the governing oppressive enslavement by the king of Egypt. I mean they were oppressed, *oppressed*. Their enslavement happened because the king of Egypt felt like the children of Israel were populating too much. So, his grand idea was to enslave them, make them work under his rule and also initiate population control. If he could mentally enslave them, then the physical bondage would be a breeze. And it worked! For so many years.

But...the more the Egyptians dominated them, the more the children of Israel grew in number. They cried out to God, and God saw their suffering and acted by sending Moses. After several encounters with Pharoah, plagues and preparation, the children of Israel left Egypt. They had protection, provision and God's presence. It was all good until Pharoah flipped the script and went after them with his army. As soon as it looked as if Pharoah were about to set it off in their camp, they started panicking. Cries rang out: "Woe is me." and "What are we going to do?" and "We told you this was going to happen!" and "Let us be slaves to the Egyptians."

Say what now?!

Let us be slaves to the Egyptians. Like, for real? At the first sign of trouble, they preferred to have gone back to slavery instead of walking in their freedom. God had shown them His hand in every aspect of Him working through Moses and in signs and wonders to show them He was working on their behalf. When it looked like it was about to go down, they forgot God's promise and His presence in the camp.

Sounds familiar? Yeah, it does. I remember first reading about the children of Israel, and I distinctly remembered how I was like, "They had all the proof they needed. Why would they turn away from God? Why would they get scared? Why would they dishonor God? Why, why, why?"

But God said, *just keep living.* I've been living, and now, I understand.

I believe you understand too. Life has a way of humbling people. Some of us have become mentally captive by the past reminders of pain and disappointment. We live in the continuous cycle of what didn't work, who hurt us, or what hurt us. I believe we help mentally oppress ourselves by reminding ourselves of the past, then we decide we don't ever want to feel that way **again** by taking the necessary steps to shield ourselves. That's one of the biggest, life-stunting mistakes to ever make.

Let me talk to you. Lean closer to the page. You are physically and spiritually delivered, but mentally, you are longing for the familiarity of bondage. It's not necessarily for the comfort, but the bondage is all you've allowed yourself to know. Freedom is yours now, and you have to move differently. The growing pains hurt; I know. Despite that, you have to keep moving forward.

Where you're going is unknown, and you don't know what awaits you. The hurdles you have to jump are foreign to you. See back in bondage, you knew the hurdles like the back of your hand. For this reason, jumping them was a breeze. The truth is you became acclimated and immune to your mental prison, so the effects of the oppression didn't quite feel oppressive anymore until God shook things up by sending someone or something to free you. Yet, deep in the recesses of your spirit, you cried out to God, and He answered. Which means, God has a plan for your life.

You deserve to be free just like the children of Israel. One thing you have to shake off is the mentality of the children of Israel. I really believe they had Stockholm syndrome. Stockholm syndrome is when the captive has developed favorable feelings towards their captor (person or situation). Retraining your brain is a must. Those first pains of discomfort will have the recently released captive feeling like, "Get somebody else to do it." It hurts, but the pain is a testament to your spirit's fight against your flesh. Let the spirit win.

No journey is without disappointment, rejection or failure. Be that as it may, whenever you do encounter setbacks of any sort, make sure your confidence is not at a deficit. Because when confidence is at a deficit, people tend to discredit their worthiness of reaching wholeness. The key to staying on the course and not allowing the past to encumber the future is by getting acquainted with the solution. You're an expert at knowing your problems inside and out. How about becoming well-versed in the solution. The solution is your trust in God.

Just as God delivered the children of Israel and gave them the protection, provision, and His presence, He is offering the same to you. All you have to do is trust Him. Place your hand in His and let Him guide you out of the mental prison that has held you back from God's best.

One more thing you need to do to remove the mental shackles. Forgive yourself, Queen. For the bad decisions. For the time wasted. For the people, places and things that kept you from God. For everything you allowed the enemy to use to condemn you. Give yourself the same grace God freely gives you every single day. LET IT GO! You have no more time to waste holding on to guilt, shame and self-recrimination. Give yourself a fresh start with God. He's not holding on to that stuff. God wants you to not just be free but to be free indeed. So many neglect to forgive themselves, and that's why many are still bound to the guilt and shame of the past. Release yourself from self-condemnation. Say aloud: *I forgive myself*. Repeat it. Feel the weight of self-disapproval lift from your shoulders. If you must, practice forgiving yourself until you *actually* forgive yourself. This is one of the most powerful liberating things you can do; this is self-care.

Your body and spirit are already liberated, and your mind should be as well. Imagine how beautiful your life will be when you allow the past to stay in the past and allow yourself to embrace healing. Imagine living your best life and the desires of your heart are laid at your feet. One day you won't have to imagine because you will have done the work.

Trust God. Unchain your mind.

It's time to move differently.

P.S. Back in June, I watched an Instagram reel of rapper, Tobe Nwigwe, and his daughter which touched my heart and reminded me of how God sees us, encourages us and protects us. Watch this visual inspiration and reminder at the link below.

https://www.instagram.com/reel/CtT5NePKRip/?igshid =MWQ1ZGUxMzBkMA==

Chapter 4

Finding Joy After Sorrow

By **Latasha Ramsey-Cyprian**

On August 15, 2007, my father passed away from a massive heart attack at the age of fifty-three. My father left behind a wife, two sons, and me-his daughter-along with three grandchildren. My life turned upside down after his unexpected death. I'll never forget the day my mother called me hysterical, telling me that my father was being rushed to the hospital after being found unconscious. I was headed home from work that day, and the hospital was in the opposite direction. I was giving a coworker a ride home when I received the phone call. My coworker tried to comfort me by telling me everything was going to be ok, but I could only think about getting to the hospital to see for myself. After dropping her off, I turned around to head to the hospital. I couldn't make it there fast enough. The forty-five-minute drive seemed as though it took me forever to get there. I prayed to God the entire ride, asking that He make a way for my father to pull through. As a child growing up, my parents taught my siblings and I about the importance of prayer. We were a closeknit family, and we attended church regularly as a family. Throughout my life, I witnessed amazing things happen for my family and others because of prayer. I strongly believed that prayers truly changed things. I was confident that by the time I made it to the hospital I would find my father in stable or fair condition. I had a lot of faith that God was going to take care of him.

Once I made it to the hospital, I raced to find my mother in the waiting room. At that time, the doctors hadn't updated her on my father's condition. A few minutes later, a doctor walked into the waiting room with a very distraught look on his face. The doctor informed my family that he and his staff did everything they could do to revive my father, but unfortunately, he did not make it. Hearing the terrible news hit like a ton of bricks. The news took the ground completely out from under me. I cried like I had never cried before. I felt as if I was in a nightmare that I wanted to wake up from. I could not process the news that I had just received. I immediately tried to console my mother, but I was just as shocked and emotional as she was. My younger brother hadn't made it to the hospital yet, and I remember calling him as he was headed to the hospital to give him the bad news. At that moment, my life completely changed. I started questioning God. How could God allow my father to die? Did God not hear my prayers to Him? What had my father done to deserve to die?

A few minutes prior to my father's death, he and my mother stopped at a grocery store to grab a few items after work. They were planning to head home and get ready for bible study. My mother stayed in the truck while he went into the store. Unfortunately, my father did not come out of the store alive. All I could think about is he was on his way to serve God that evening, and he didn't live to do so. I was hurt, angry, confused and mad. So many emotions were going through my mind as the doctor walked out of the waiting room after telling us the horrific news. I was broken, weak and sick to my stomach. At that moment, I lost all confidence in God. God had never let me down until that point, and I could not understand why He allowed this to happen. I was twenty-seven years old at the time of my father's death, and I depended on him for guidance and wisdom even at that age. What was I going to do now? How was I going to get through life? I wanted to completely shut down. That was impossible because I had a one-year-old daughter who needed me to care for her. I knew I had to be strong for my mother as we grieved the loss of our backbone. That day was the worst day of my life.

As the days passed after my father's death, I grew more and more sad. Reality hit me at my father's funeral that he was gone forever, and I knew life would not be the same. I had no desire to live at that point. Life wasn't meaningful anymore. All I could think about was how God failed me. I never put my confidence in man, but I always had confidence in God. I learned how emotionally challenging death could be during my grieving process. People would try to console me by saying "He's in a better place" and "God makes no mistakes." I was not trying to hear any of that. In my opinion, it was a mistake because my father should have still been alive.

I experienced several stages of grief. My first stage of grief was disbelief. After a week of bereavement leave, I immediately returned to work. I tried to stay busy and not think about my father. That was impossible because everything reminded me of him. I was overwhelmed with emotions. I tried praying to God for strength, and I immediately would get upset. In my mind, God no longer heard my prayers and felt there was no point in prayer. Grief disrupted my spiritual discipline. The second stage of grief that I experienced was depression. I bottled my emotions and that made it worse for me mentally and physically. When I was alone, I would cry, and there were many nights I cried myself to sleep. I would set my alarm clock to wake up twenty minutes early for work because my eyes would be puffy from crying the night before. Applying a cold compress to my eyes to help the swelling go away became a normal morning routine. I started drinking frequently as an external way to cope. Drinking seemed to calm me at first, but as weeks passed, alcohol perpetuated my grief. It was harder for me to process my emotions, and I was still sad.

The sadness and unresolved feelings then turned into more anger. I was still upset with God, and I was even mad at my father for leaving his family. I questioned if my father would have eaten healthier, went to the doctor more and exercised regularly, would he still be alive? I went back and forth with this stage, and I felt my feelings were justified. I began to feel jealous of people who still had their father. Life didn't seem fair, and I only wanted to do the bare minimum. During that time, I got frustrated with people easily. The smallest things irritated me, and I didn't want to talk to friends. A social life did not exist, and there was no desire to have one. There was no way I could gather with friends and have a good time while I was completely broken. Trying to be strong for my mother was a challenge because I was weak myself; however, I knew my father would want me to offer my support to her. I stopped attending church regularly. When I did attend church, I wasn't paying attention to the sermon because I doubted God, and my faith had wavered and weakened.

Months after my father passed, I finally accepted his passing. Society places a lot of pressure on people to get over death easily. My father was present for every stage of my life, and his death was a tough pill to swallow once reality sunk in. We are taught to embrace death as a part of life, however, it does not take the pain away. I missed my relationship with God, and I knew I had to re-establish my relationship with Him for my sanity. There was no way I could live the remainder of my life with the amount of anger I had in my heart. My power had diminished, and I was severely depressed. There was so much focus on the past that I could not think about the future. My father's death was a transformative event. Growing up in church, I heard countless sermons on how fragile life is. His death showed me that life can end at any moment without notice.

Apologizing to God for losing confidence and faith in Him for months was necessary. During my talk with God, I specifically stated how my emotions allowed me to stop believing in Him. I admitted to what I did, and I asked Him to forgive me and to give me the strength to move forward with my life. For months I prayed to God to send me a sign that my father was ok. I knew he was in Heaven because of the life that he lived on Earth, but I didn't have the chance to say goodbye to him. On my twenty-eighth birthday, I had a dream about my father. It was the first dream of him that I remembered having since his passing. In the dream, he seemed in great spirit, and he had his normal big smile that could light up an entire room. He stood there smiling at me for a brief period of time, then he waved and turned around and walked away. The dream woke me out of my sleep. I was emotional yet happy at the same time. The dream was the confirmation I needed that he was ok and that I needed to go on with my life. My interpretation of the dream was that he was happy and in a better place. At that moment I faced the fact that I would never physically see him again on Earth, but I would see him again one day. I had to get my life back on track to find solace and comfort in what I once relied on to get me through.

Regaining my confidence and faith in God required me to reconnect with Him. When I broke down several times asking God for forgiveness, I always felt calmness come over me. I was reminded that God will meet us where we are, and He won't shame or condemn us. God was my shoulder to lean on, and He was my strength when I was weak. When I went through the different stages of grief, God was with me the entire time. When I lost faith in Him, He was still there. The more I started reaching out to God in prayer, the more He comforted and encouraged me. Grief is painful, and I learned how to cope with my emotions and pain by trusting in God. The tragic event of losing my father allowed me to grow in faith, and I got closer to God. Praying helped lift me out of depression, and my heart became softer.

Hebrews 10:35-36 states, *"Cast not away therefore your confidence, which hath great recompence of reward. For ye have need of patience, that, after ye have done the will of God, ye might receive the promise."* I honored my journey, and it has been of brokenness and healing. There were many memories I had of my father from when I was a little girl up until his passing. I was blessed to have those memories. I started to treasure the relationships I had with my mother and family. Knowing that my father had a relationship with God allowed me to deal with his death better. Had he not had that relationship, I would be worried. I know he is standing before the throne of God singing and rejoicing and experiencing joy and peace like he's never known.

Knowing that my father is in Heaven gives me joy even though I still miss him terribly. I try not to take people for granted, and I spend time with those that I love as much as I can. I don't put off things for tomorrow that I can do today. At some point in life, I will lose more people close to me. I can only hope that when the time comes, their loss will be bittersweet and not just bitter. I will never be the same person that I was before my father's death, but the best way to move beyond grief is to process it. His death taught me a lot about life, love and healing. My father deeply touched my life, and I am grateful for the twenty-seven years God gave me with him. I realized that God does not make mistakes because He is the truth, He has a plan, and He has never broken a promise. I will continue to trust God because I have found joy in my soul again.

Latasha Ramsey-Cyprian, a mother of two daughters, is a native of Louisiana. Latasha works professionally in HR. She received her MBA from Louisiana State University-Shreveport and received an honorary doctorate degree in Philosophy from T.I.U.A. Latasha is a Bestselling Author, Credit Repair Strategist, International Speaker, Educator and Certified Life Coach. Latasha is the owner of Optimum Life Enterprises LLC and Optimum Life Credit Solutions. She is Louisiana State Chair for G100 Oneness & Wisdom, board president of Catch My Heart Outreach non-profit organization, member of Gamma Phi Delta Sorority, Inc and member of Tangipahoa Regional Black Business Chamber of Commerce. She is a member of Tangipahoa Professional Women and member of National Black MBA Association, Inc. Latasha is Brand Ambassador for Expressions of Humanity, the Black Family Magazine and TAPN2U Peace Partner. Latasha believes that the best way to find yourself is to lose yourself in the service of others.

To connect with Latasha by email:
info@optimumlifecreditsolutions.com.
To view/order her eBooks, financial planners and books
visit: https://payhip.com/OptimumLifeEnterprisesLLC
Website: www.optimumlifecreditsolutions.com

Chapter 5

Delivered But Mute

Gag Order

Ever come across a person who in the past suffered a traumatic event(s) and they didn't want to talk about it? Because to them, dredging up those memories can be triggering. In essence, they've put a gag order on themselves, and known to some and unbeknownst to others, this is also a form of bondage.

When a person who has been waiting for the day to be freed from whatever type of situation which imprisoned them, they enthusiastically embrace freedom and block their mind to what they left behind. They don't want reminders of the real thing or anything similar. Freedom is theirs, and they're not going back to what was, so don't even ask about it. Totally understandable, though...there are some unresolved issues at play. Not to say the person isn't grateful to be delivered, but also showing God one's gratitude by glorifying His name is the act of telling others what He has done.

Back in 2005, Hurricane Katrina ravaged parts of Louisiana and parts of Mississippi. My family and I evacuated to Dallas, TX the day before the hurricane hit land. It was a wise choice. Though we escaped the hurricane, we didn't escape the aftermath. It all became real once we returned home days later. We suffered through having no electricity, no air conditioning, no generator nor gas for a generator, no cell service and no running water while the heat and humidity raged furiously outside. Before we left home, we thoroughly cleaned up. My mother left a new Glade plug-in with a small built-in fan running. The scent smelled so good, and that's the first smell we encountered upon walking in the house.

We endured the discomfort of the separation from our daily comforts for almost three weeks. God allowed us to find a generator, and things slowly got better. The water was turned back on after a week. After two and a half weeks, we got our electricity back. During recovery and cleanup in our town and individual homes, we got up early every morning and went in search of gas, supplies, food and ice. Things eventually returned to normal.

I knew that time in my life was difficult, and I really didn't realize how much that had an impact on me emotionally. I knew the physical aspects of it; I had an allergic reaction that spanned a few months. That was easier to deal with because I could physically see the problem. Mentally, I didn't see what was lingering. A smell triggered me. One day after cleaning up, my mother decided to use the same scented Glade plug-in to freshen up the house. Once that smell permeated my nose, I grew sick to my stomach. The plug-in was immediately trashed. It not only triggered me but triggered her as well. Although the scent was in the trash, psychologically, the scent was imprinted in my mind, bringing along the memories of Hurricane Katrina.

Living in the gulf coast, my area is prone to hurricanes and tropical storms. We can't allow ourselves to be stuck in fear over the weather and the devastation it sometimes brings. I knew I couldn't allow myself to be triggered because other storms were coming. How did I overpower the negative memories? I let the memories flow, and I allowed myself to see the blessing in the storm. Hurricane

Katrina taught me how to prepare, how to take alternate routes, how to adjust in uncomfortable situations, and basically, how to survive. Not only that, but my family also didn't lose anything substantial except for our food, which was easily replaced. Financial blessings came our way, and everything we needed, God made sure we received it.

God doesn't orchestrate pain, but He does strategize it. God always has a plan to get us out of painful situations and to use them to show His providence. When we tell people how we got over, we glorify Him. Just think about the woman at the well (John 4). She was a Samaritan woman with a bad reputation, low social standing and living in sin. Jesus approached her one day, ran down the tea about her life and offered her living water- she accepted! Not only did the Samaritan woman have an up-close encounter with Jesus, but she was also delivered from sin. Jesus told her, "Girl, tell people about me." And she did. Her obedience and telling everyone about what He did for her delivered many in her town. The scripture in verse thirty-nine says, *"Many of the Samaritans from that town believed in him because of the woman's testimony..."*

I'm not trying to downplay the trauma anyone has experienced. I do encourage you to deal with your past in the healthiest way possible. God didn't deliver you for you to remain mute about His glorious works. No, you don't have to give intimate details about your life, your pain. You *are* responsible for advancing God's kingdom. That universal purpose has not been preempted from your life or mine because of things that happened to us. Although a choice, it is your responsibility as a believer. And sharing your testimony will encourage deliverance for the next person.

Please don't let your past keep your mouth closed. Free yourself from the bondage of bad memories and triggers. Sing your deliverance for those with an ear to hear. Those who want it will accept it. Addressing the pain will hurt, however, on the other side of the pain is unadulterated joy and peace.

Therapy works, and prayer changes things.

Lift the gag order.

Chapter 6

Taking My Power Back

By **LaToya Nicole**

While on my journey of reclaiming my throne, I learned that allowing others to dictate my life was destroying my confidence. I gave my power away whenever I went against my desires to appease people. I never felt good enough during those times, so others' opinions affected how I felt about myself even further. Most of my feelings towards myself were based on how others treated me, leading me on emotional roller coasters that were hard to break free from. I would alter my goals if people I respected rejected me. That is one reason why it took me so long to become an author. I remember sharing the desire to write with a relative. When I did not get the feedback I sought, I suppressed the dream and chased other things, trying to make my family proud of me.

At the most impressionable time of my life, I was abused and made to feel like I was a problem. Never validated by my mother, I learned to become someone else and people pleased to protect my feelings, but it only made things worse. While I envisioned different responses that would make me feel good about myself, I received responses that further destroyed me. To avoid backlash, I took note of what upset my mother and did everything I could to fix it before I became target practice. Even when I did not want to, I did my chores and helped my brother with his homework. As a young child, I learned to clean and organize well, so I would have the entire house clean only to be scolded anyway for one minor thing out of place. When my brother failed, I was blamed for not helping him. Somehow, anytime something was wrong, I was accused, but when things were going well, there was never any praise for me. I internalized this as not being good enough. My life became one of over giving, over loving, and overstaying only to be left feeling the same way my mother made me feel as a child. When I realized what was happening, my confidence level dropped below the bottom of the barrel. I lost hope in everything, and I did not want to do anything. I lost myself in trying to be accepted. Time and time again, life proved that my family was not interested in me and what I had going on if it did not benefit them, so I moved from needing their approval to that of friends and partners. Unfortunately, I moved from bad to worse. My insecurity in myself and my abilities opened the door to a level of self-sabotage I was desperate to escape for over a decade.

Although the slaps of reality to my face were hard enough to snap out of it, I stuck around people who put me down repeatedly. Christian friends always had "a word" until it came to pass in my life, and then I got the stank eye. If they weren't doing better, there would be no celebration for me. I will never forget the time I taught dance at my former church. I have always been a person to go the extra mile and learn everything I need to know. I enrolled in Eagle's Institute to pour only the best about the art of dance into my students. I did not want them to dance just to do something; I wanted them to learn how to minister in God's presence. Other dancers I knew from other ministries had exposed me to so much, and I wanted the children of Interdenominational Faith Assembly to become aware of how much more there was. Extremely excited about this venture, I shared it with two people I trusted. One in particular asked, "What are you doing that for?" Her response took me aback, and I almost lost it.

Hearing her say that the way she said it triggered me so badly. All I could think about was how my family would say things to discourage me and shut me down. There I was decades later feeling like I did when I would share ideas with my mother or grandmother, only to feel defeated. All of those emotions surfaced, and I felt like a little girl longing for the acceptance of her mother. Mother wounds were at the root of my low self-worth and lack of confidence. However, I continued with my decision to attend Eagle's Institute. I went home as always, curled in a fetal position, and wept. I had to swallow that no one supported what I was doing. Many in the church questioned why I was chosen to teach and not others who had been in the ministry since they were children. On one hand, the pastor's choice was questioned, and on the other, so was my desire to learn how to teach and lead properly. It was one thing after another until I detached and moved on, but it took a lot to get me to a place of letting go.

From childhood until my thirties, my confidence was shredded like it had been inserted in a paper shredder. There were so many loose pieces to heal that I never thought I could put them together to make sense of the outcomes in my life. Rebuilding myself to go after what I wanted after numerous attacks on my esteem, which negatively impacted my confidence, seemed impossible. It was hard for me to trust or believe in anything. I showed myself as supportive, yet I had no support. I was emotionally wounded, sincerely not having anyone in my corner like I had seen them be there for others. No matter where I was, I never fit in, nearly destroying me. I had to decide between two choices: detach and live my life with or without the support of others or continue to self-destruct, waiting on others to validate me. The choice was mine, and I had to choose me.

As I journeyed through life, I noticed the same spirit in those from my childhood I dated in the men I chose. I allowed severely emotionally damaged men to shatter my confidence, from one broken situation to another. Serial cheaters with mommy issues took their frustration with their mothers out on me, resulting in internal chaos I had to sort and declutter. Sometimes I looked at myself in the mirror and hated my appearance. I was mad at them and myself for allowing it to get that far. Being cheated on and taking them back further stripped me of my confidence as I saw the pattern in the women they chose, and they looked nothing like me. To everyone around me, I walked tall and held it together, but when I was alone at night, I cried myself to sleep many times. One toxic relationship after the other significantly impacted my mental health. The criticism, belittling, and manipulation caused emotional distress, leading to not only blows to my esteem but also anxiety and depression I battled, *Alone In The Dark.*

By now, you see how lacking confidence had affected every area of my life. One blow compromised everything I desired to be and do. Where I once thrived, I questioned my ability. When I started to regain my voice, I began to shrink back. The clothes and shoes I once felt terrific in, I no longer did. My work reflected how I felt within; it even manifested through my skin. I had to heal from how my family broke me and how I furthered it, choosing friends and men just like them. Every insult revealed areas of low confidence. The smallest of things offended me. My wounds were loud. I could not hear myself over them.

There was a lot of work to do. I had to go back to the beginning, understand where it all started and why I responded the way I did.

When surrounded by others who are not confident in their ability, they will do everything they can to bring you down to a point beneath them. They thrive off of that, knowing there is someone who feels exactly like they do or worse. That saying "hurt people, hurt people" is true. Damaged people, damage people, and insecure people break other people's confidence. These people are family, friends, co-workers, lovers, etc. Once I understood and accepted this truth, I could tear down self-sabotaging thought processes and rebuild my life. I sought help healing the origin to move past people who projected their insecurities onto me. I had to go back to never being validated by my mother or being seen by my family. Family breaks us, so we never get the confidence to walk away. They want you always to need them.

Allow me to encourage you that it is never too late to take your power back and reclaim your throne of confidence. Commit to yourself to live your desired life, not the one suggested. You will take the driver's seat rather than the passenger seat. My years in therapy helped me get to the root of why I repeatedly gave my power away. I stripped away everything that gave me a false sense of confidence. I may have worn the highest heel and the most makeup, but I felt low. There was a time when you would not catch me in a flat shoe, but as I healed, I no longer found it necessary to wear them. I was finally confident in who I am. It has been years since I started this work, but I consistently try to regain and maintain momentum. As I peel back layers daily, I am taking my rightful position back. I am learning who LaToya is and what she likes. My passions are being discovered, and I am living on my terms. What someone else feels is best for me based on their beliefs is no longer a factor in my decision-making.

Ways To Take Your Power Back & Reclaim Your Throne:

- Start saying no when you do not want to go.
- Talk to a counselor.
- Be gentle with yourself.
- Stop pretending to be someone you are not.
- Acknowledge how you feel.

- Learn to detach when it is no longer emotionally safe.
- Build with people who appreciate you.
- Set achievable goals and stick to them.
- Read self-improvement books.

Journal Prompts

Talk about two experiences that robbed you of your confidence? How was your life impacted? Did you find your way back? Does the sting of what happened affect your decisions today?

____

____

____

____

____

What does confidence mean to you?

____

____

Were you confident as a child?

Were you validated as a child? Were your accomplishments celebrated? Do you celebrate your accomplishments now?

What would you stop doing if you had more confidence?

In what area of your life do you need more confidence? How would your life change if you had it?

What do you love about yourself?

LaToya Nicole is a bestselling author, passionate coach, consultant, and business owner with a zest for success. Within her businesses, she holds multiple certifications that enhance clients' lives meaningfully and authentically. LaToya understands the importance of emotional intelligence and optimal mental health and provides impressive insight rooted in her education and success in overcoming life's challenges.

As a Certified: Therapon Belief Therapist, Life Coach, Journal Therapist, Mindfulness Coach, Business Coach, and Organizer, LaToya can help you go from goals to accomplished by healing blocks organizationally, emotionally, mentally, or physically. She does this through writing, which is why she created Unaltered Voices.

LaToya has suffered from adverse childhood experiences, robbed of her voice, and made to feel her existence was a burden. She has made it her life's work to help others heal and become better versions of themselves.

LaToya's literary works include:

Alone In the Dark, My Battle with Depression

From Pit to Purpose, Recovering After Emotional Setbacks Workbook

Tell Your Story Unaltered, Writing Your First Draft Made Easy

Journal Therapy, Therapeutic Writing Workbook

Several collaborative book projects, including:

The Coaches Connect Volume One

The Coaches Connect Volume II

If These Walls Could Talk Stories of Surviving Childhood Trauma

The Miseducation of Becoming an Adult

Sisters Inspire Sisters Vol II

& More

Follow LaToya On Social Media:

Instagram: @iam_latoyanicole

For interviews and other bookings, contact: info@latoyanicoleinc.com

Website: www.latoyanicoleinc.com

Blog: www.healthruwriting.net

Chapter 7

Affirming the Queen Within

Scepter In Hand

Rebuilding your confidence takes practice, takes intentionality, and dare I say consistency with a big dash of certainty. Comparison has held women in the tightest chokehold for ages. We wish we had less of this or more of that like the next woman, making us feel inferior because we judge ourselves against other women who actually have insecurities as well. Not only do we critique ourselves, we have to listen to the vitriol from the "social media experts" and "podcast experts" (insert an eyeroll here) on how women should act, think, treat their men, fit a certain physical aesthetic and every other thing they can think of to hold us to this super feminine standard. Then the glorified surgically enhanced bodies adds to the fray. It's crazy!

Allowing the double-minded ways of the world to convince you that you are somehow lacking just doesn't sit right with me. I pray it doesn't sit right with you either. You know, I had to get to a point where I mentally conceded how I had unnecessarily exhausted myself with the contemptuous voice I allowed to fester and grow out of control. The contemptuous voice that didn't matter and had no legitimacy in who God has created me to be. That same voice has invaded the emotions of women globally. That voice must be stopped and its falsehood exposed.

On this journey of reclaiming your Queendom, you are going to have to affirm yourself. Your confidence has got to be at a level where it can sustain any opposition. Of course, there will be days when you may feel down because there is no guarantee that a faithful person can't feel depressed or afraid. However, your conviction has to outweigh the depression and the fear so you can press through on your faith journey.

Here's what you have to do to affirm the Queen within:

1. Read and apply Philippians 4:8 which says, "And now, dear brothers and sisters, one final thing. Fix your thoughts on what is true, and honorable, and right, and pure, and lovely, and admirable. Think about things that are excellent and worthy of

praise." Meaning stop rehearsing those old, tired lines that old, tired played out voice has told you over the years. Practice thinking the truth.

2. Gain the clarity you need to bolster your confidence by actually believing the pure thoughts you've been practicing. Belief is a choice. Your choice.

3. Verbalize your thoughts and beliefs. Speak aloud what you are now and who you will become in the future. Call those things that are not as though they were. Replace "I'm not" and "I can't" with "I am" and "I can" and then put icing on the cake by backing it up with scripture.

30-day Affirmation Challenge:

Practice saying aloud while staring your regal self in the mirror...I am more than a conqueror. I am special. I am blessed. I am capable. I am strong. I am enough. I am intelligent. I am a blessing. I am redeemed. I am beautiful. I have an abundant life. I am healed. I am successful. I have a hope and a future.

Freestyle and add more to the list. You know exactly the life you have envisioned for yourself. Rebuilding your confidence will help you to do things you've shied away from doing and take offered opportunities you would've allowed to bypass you in the past. You can be scared but still-at the same time-dominate the assignment or goal before you. Knowing God, knowing who you are in Him and knowing you can be vulnerable with God is the embodiment of confidence.

This is a process, but I know you will come out on the other side with your crown secure and scepter in hand, ready to rule your Queendom with confidence.

Chapter 8

Godly Confidence: You Are Enough

By **Janice Prescott**

When I was younger, one of the things my mom always said to me was not to live my life in a cage. I wasn't quite sure what she meant until I got older. Eventually, the statement began to weigh on me, because when I thought about my life, I did not understand where I was caging myself. Eventually, through much soul searching and the help of the Holy Spirit, I came to the conclusion that I was not being my authentic self, and I was hiding parts of myself from others. I wanted to avoid getting further hurt by painful circumstances. I also realized that this affected my confidence and how I was living my life because we are not just caged by our circumstances, but also by the way we respond to these circumstances.

I used to be somewhat shy and was picked on when I was younger. We were the first Black family where we lived after immigrating to Canada. My parents worked hard and were heavily into church. I had good friends, but not everybody was nice. As I got older, I realized firsthand what it meant to lose trust in people. Being an introvert who enjoyed her own company, I just naturally kept to those spaces I knew well, like family and church. Although I had a good group of friends, as time went on, I found that people could be quite cruel when you're not part of the cool crowd. Interacting was sometimes difficult, and I constantly compared myself to others. I often tried to be who people thought I was just to be accepted. I began to resent the entire process of fitting in. I felt others took advantage of me because I appeared to be quiet. However, when crossed, I could definitely tell you about yourself. The truth was that inside l was angry and frustrated. l really wanted a place to belong and hated when those close to me or those with authority over me tried to diminish and tell me who they thought l was, even to this day.

I realized that my silence wasn't helping me. I could not hide any more. Thankfully, the Lord gave me ways to be more outgoing and confident. It all started with Church and some advice from really great spiritual mentors. I became the leader of a few ministries where I interacted with all different types of people on a regular basis. I also started to write and share my devotionals. The feedback was largely positive, so my confidence grew. In addition, the Lord helped me find my gift. He encouraged me to encourage others. He showed me that I had the gift of exhortation and that I could pour into people the way He was pouring into me.

When I struggled or felt that I was out of my league, God told me I was enough. That became the theme of my life. I even used this mantra as a theme for one of the Youth days I planned at church. It was a blessing to encourage others with the truths that the Lord was teaching me. Now, l don't accept baseless criticism based only on the categories that people want to put me in. I say "no" to people who are more content if I stay quiet and don't like my message. The Lord and the Spirit convict and guide me, and l have confidence in that. I am never alone. God has done so many wonderful things for me, and He has blessed me with the ability to be myself and accept myself. I can just be me, and I like what He's done in me so far.

Because of this, I can accept others, be kind and encouraging, as well as take their own past and painful experiences into account to walk in their shoes. I realize not everyone is going to love me. However, as long as God does, all things will work out.

What is Godly confidence? We are daughters of Zion. Children of the most high. Our confidence is in God's love for us and seeing ourselves the way He sees us. Life is about accepting ourselves as we are and not comparing ourselves to others. I reject living the way society says is best or within people's incorrect categorizations. I am not just Black, or a woman, or a Christian. I am the sum total of all these things.

Having an intimate relationship with God and the Holy Spirit is the only way to have Godly confidence and the only way that lasts. Our confidence comes from knowing God's got it. His love covers us even through our constant mistakes. We must seek Him, trust in His guidance, and ask for His forgiveness.

Confidence can come from our experiences and routines over time. However, belief in yourself and wisdom go hand in hand. The only way to be discerning and sure of your future is to turn your life, emotions, and endeavors over to the one who sees all. When we constantly trust that God will give us the wisdom, knowledge and understanding for every situation, then we experience confidence in Him and increased belief in what He can do through us to bless others. Peace and joy in His presence can truly be ours because we have faith and knowledge of His relationship with us, what He has done for us, what He is doing now and what He will do in the future. If you want Godly confidence, you can start by giving your issues over to God and following the steps below.

- Let the past go. Don't worry about your incorrect decisions from years gone by.
- Forgive yourself. Trust in God, and let Him heal you.
- Open the Word, and see what God says about you. Repeat it until you believe it.
- Walk humbly with your God.
- Put your trust in God, and truly let Him lead.
- Don't be afraid to try things, and don't be afraid to fail.

- Worship Him in gratitude for what He is doing and what He will do.

Originally from the lovely Island of St. Vincent and the Grenadines, in the West Indies, **Janice** migrated to Canada with her family at an early age. She discovered a love for words and writing in grade school and enjoys a career in the Information Technology Industry. Janice also endeavors to share God's Love with others through her devotionals. This provides her with a unique vantage point to share what God has done through her writing and now as part of the Queen's Confidence Anthology. She is also an English tutor and founder of Faith Factor Editing. Her hope is that you will be encouraged as you read and draw nearer to God.

Don't Go Back

His Sovereignty

"So let us come boldly to the throne of our gracious God. There we will receive his mercy, and we will find grace to help us when we need it most." -Hebrews 4:16 NLT

Royal Blunders

I can't tell you how many mistakes I've made on my faith journey. They are too innumerable to count, but they've all been beneficial to my growth. Would I know what it's like to be right if I never made a mistake? No, I wouldn't. My perspective would always be one-sided. I thank God for my errors. Had I not experienced failure, I wouldn't be able to teach the next person. I wouldn't have the depth of gratitude I have for God, and I wouldn't be able to appreciate my life. In order to learn and grow, you need to make mistakes.

When life happens, it becomes easy to fall off the rails emotionally and spiritually. No, the reaction to pain, disappointment and the illusion of failure is not a planned reaction. Whenever you sustain the brunt of any type of setback, you have to be careful in how you work through your emotions and how adjust in your faith. Always remind yourself that emotions are temporary, and making permanent decisions while you're upset can cause disastrous consequences. Making decisions when you're emotional means you are relying on yourself to make informed decisions without the influence of God. Can you see how doing so could cause an unwanted problem in your life? Take the time to calm down and reevaluate the situation. Emotions will fool a person into believing all is lost. Not so because God wouldn't put you on a path destined for failure.

Also, settling in your faith during those tough times will help you settle your emotions. Go to God when everything seems confusing and overwhelming. When the mirage of failure looks certain. Praise and worship will get your mind back on track. The longer you prolong going to the problem solver, the longer your internal conflict will rage. Even if the fault lies with you. God can make sense of the situation and impart the strategies needed to circumvent the "end" you anticipated.

Perhaps you do allow your emotions to get the best of you, stalling your correspondence with God. It happens, and the occurrence is understandable. If it does happen, don't stay there. Wallowing in an injured mindset for too long is an impediment to your process. Some people hastily abort the process before they reach the promise because they fall back to the old mindset. Pity parties commence and it's downhill from there. BUT you **shall not** permeate your progress with old habits and thoughts God has delivered you from. You **shall** continue to walk in deliverance. Queen of mistakes is not your label. Redeemed, set free, chosen, holy and special are just a few classifications which speak loudly to the masses about your character and your expected destination.

Blunders are just blunders, then there's the blunders you cause. If by chance you facilitated the mistake, the promise is still yours. God didn't take it away because you didn't perform perfectly. He already knew you were going to mess up, and since He already knew, He waits for you to come to Him to regroup. You and God got to get to the root to answer why. Knowing your why will help you admit your role in what went wrong. Take accountability whether your actions were intentional or not and forgive yourself.

Succeeding the first step of accountability, resolve within to resist making repetitive mistakes. Listen, for some of us, it takes a minute for us to stop making the same mistakes. Others can quit cold turkey. Us slow learners have to process it out. Create an action plan and implement said action plan to help you avoid the drawback of the same setback. Cut out the distractions, develop discipline, maintain consistency, take a course, get a mentor- whatever is needed. Long as you continue to try and learn, the day you can advance to the next level will be a joyous one when you can look back and rejoice over how far God brought you.

Just a few short years ago, when I made a mistake, I'd be like, "What's wrong with me? I'm such a loser. Why can't I get it right? I don't deserve to have..." Talk about a throwback pity party, inviting that old mindset back in a space it no longer deserved to occupy. And for a time, I refused to move forward in my endeavors because I coached myself into believing that I was unworthy. I self-sabotaged a lot until I realized the time wasted and dreams yet fulfilled. My self-imposed stagnation sent me right back to God so He could help me get back on track.

Avoid getting sucked into the way you used to think by sustaining the renewed mind you worked hard to develop and get through the mistakes when they occur with God's help. Mistakes are inevitable, but your growth should be too.

Don't you dare go back.

Chapter 10

Walk In Your Truth

By **Colleen Williams Rennie**

"You gain strength, courage, and confidence by every experience in which you really stop to look fear in the face. You are able to say to yourself, 'I have lived through this horror. I can take the next thing that comes along.' You must do the thing you think you cannot do."
-Eleanor Roosevelt

Many men and women lack confidence and that is because of what was instilled in their minds, how they were raised or something they have experienced. Confidence is like a golden key to open the doors to your future, and once you have that key in your hand, you hold the door to a world you never knew existed. Just like a great resume opens doors, having a great cover letter can get you the job. Knowing your worth is one thing, but having self-confidence in yourself takes the cake. Be bold, be brave, be open, be who you know you were meant to be.

I was raised in a dysfunctional family. I'm sure a lot of us can relate to that. I was always the black sheep of the family, especially with my sister. There was always a competition between us. I knew for a fact my mother liked her more than me because she was light skinned and prettier, while I was dark skinned. I felt like I was Cinderella, and my sister was the ugly stepsister. I didn't feel pretty, and nothing I did was right in my mother's eyes. The way I dressed, or should I say the things my mother would make me wear, I became a target for others to laugh at. I had low self-esteem that carried into my teenage years. When I went to high school, I would see other children wearing nice clothes and getting compliments; they were part of the popular crowd. I was always wearing hand-me-down clothes from the thrift store (although now it's my favorite place to go). I didn't feel good about myself back then. If you followed the entire story about Cinderella, you would notice along the way even though she wasn't treated fair, she was kind and very determined. Cinderella had favor and courage, and she pushed through knowing and having the confidence in herself that she was going to win at the end.

After I went out on my own, I had to work hard to regain my self-confidence. I built up enough courage to start dating. My first partner was a narcissist. He constantly abused me verbally and made me lose the confidence that I worked so hard to rebuild. I always walked with my head down, believing every word he drilled in it. I remembered one time I had a speaking engagement, and my boyfriend and I went to the mall to get an outfit. I went to try it on, and I showed him how I looked in the outfit. Without any thought, he said, "You are so ugly." I was so shocked because he said it loud and boldly in front of everyone, and it was unexpected. A few people heard him, but the guy who worked in the fitting room area said to him, "Yo don't call her ugly. She's a beautiful black Queen." While they were going back and forth, I put the outfit back and walked away. I was so embarrassed. The guy yelled out to me, "Yo Queen, you deserve better." That's when I put on my invisible crown and remembered who I was.

We got back to his house, and that incident from the mall continued. It turned into domestic violence. So not only was I living in fear, I had low self-esteem, no confidence in myself, and self-doubt silently crept in. I told him I would be right back. I hopped on the train and came back home. I blocked him and kept it moving. Because if we had just started dating and he could disrespect me in public, I didn't want to wait around to see what he was going to do behind closed doors. During our short time together, I was controlled, gaslighted, and manipulated. I was reminded daily that I was ugly and no one would ever want me. I was able to break free from him, and I took that time to rebuild my confidence once again. I knew my worth, I knew I wanted to be better, I deserved better and I wanted to do better despite my past.

I went to church one Sunday as usual. That particular morning, they were reading from Hebrews 10:35 -36. As I looked down in the bible to follow, a teardrop fell from my eyes when I read those words. *"Therefore, do not throw away your confidence, which has a great reward. For you need endurance, so that when you have done the will of God you may receive what is promised."* I felt that was God who whispered in my ear that *"He got me."* I knew that was Him letting me know I would be ok, and my tears quickly turned into a smile. He reminded me that I am fearfully and wonderfully made in His image, and if you know God as I do, then you should know He doesn't make mistakes.

From that moment forward, I regained my confidence. Once again, I started believing in myself and knowing what God had for me is for me. My mindset changed right away. God ignited the fire in me to step out on faith and be the confident woman I am today, and trust me, if He can do it for me, I know He can do it for you. I did not become confident overnight. It took me a while to get here. I had to put in a lot of work, because if you want anything out of life, you have to put in the work and go for it.

Confidence has many levels. I was a 5th grade teacher, and I saw most of my female students were following the trends that they saw on social media. I had to remind them; they didn't have to expose their body to send a message. It was ok to be confident in themselves. I taught them to know their worth. I reminded them that confidence is not in their clothes, but it is in what they do, who they are, and how they feel about themselves.

Let's talk a little bit about fear, and you will see how fear and confidence go hand in hand. When you focus on fear, it becomes your reality. Fear is something you are afraid of. Some people are afraid of heights (like flying) or walking over a high bridge (like me), but when you remove fear out the way and replace it with confidence, you can do anything you put your mind to. Now if I would have allowed my fear to get in the way, where would I be now? I would not be the confident woman I am today.

Confidence is the key, confidence starts with you, confidence starts with me, and confidence looks good on everyone.

(C) Confidence is accepting yourself for who you are and not trying to be someone you are not.

(O) Only you can make yourself happy, and gain confidence daily.

(N) Never give up.

(F) Find five things right now about yourself to take with you before you step out the door. If you can't find 5 things, here you go: faithful, fabulous, fantastic, flawless, and fierce. Thank me later.

(I) Inhale Confidence (breathe in) and I exhale doubt

and fear (breathe out.)

(D) Don't you ever let anyone tell you differently. Prove them wrong.

(E) Every morning you wake up, look in the mirror, and say one positive thing about yourself.

(N) Never forget how important you are.

(T) Tell God thank you.

(I) "I am" are the most powerful words to empower yourself. I am Confident.

(S) STOP what you're doing, look in the mirror, and smile

(S) Self-confidence comes from knowing you can succeed.

(H) Hold your head up high and remember everything you worked on to get to where you are today.

(E) Each one of us must confront our fears. We must come face to face with them.

Be confident enough so when you step into a room, everyone can see it on your face. So come here, hold my hand. I'll be your accountability partner, and we can go on this wonderful journey together. Trust me, when you get there, you will not want to go back.

Colleen Williams Rennie is a 2x bestselling author. She is a mother, wife, soccer coach, motivational speaker, and advocate for domestic violence.

When she is not writing she loves reading.

She can be reached:

Email- colleenwilliamsrennie2023@gmail.com

Facebook- Colleen Williams Rennie

Instagram- Colleen Williams Rennie

Chapter 11

Royal Decree

Reign

Your reign is dependent upon you being responsible for your Queendom, walking in freedom, lifting the gag order, affirming yourself, building your Queendom, and moving on from mistakes. These processes are capable of happening simultaneously, though one or more areas may be further advanced than others, which means you will be reigning and growing at the same time. If you are reigning and growing concurrently, please guard your heart so as to not allow imposter syndrome and feelings of inadequacy invade your reign.

Whenever you get to this final, continuous stage of recovering your throne, your mental, physical and spiritual being is prompt to exercise the sovereign power bestowed upon you by God himself.

It is here the Queen knows reigning is her birthright when: A steady, judicious mindset has evolved. A new graceful stride has emerged, and a firm iron fist is ready for action (her excellence knucketh if ye bucketh). Delicate yet conquering feet are always poised to step on the neck of any opposition with learned patience, grace and wisdom. A scepter held by the faithful hands of its resplendent Queen knows when to move on behalf of her Queendom. She is confident. Confident is she.

Issue yourself a royal decree (order given by the Queen). Set attainable boundaries, goals and non-negotiables for yourself.

- I will not ever again disrespect my Heavenly Father again by doubting what He has already said about me.
- I chose to see, believe and accept every good thing about myself, and I will improve in the areas that need work.
- I will continue to better myself. I will educate myself.
- I won't cheapen or lessen my crowned title to meet anyone's approval.

- I will be my own hype woman if no one else chooses to be. Participation from others in said hypeness is allowed but not needed.

- I will finish what I started.

- I will pray about the opportunities presented to me and about the people who present those opportunities, and I will have the strength to accept what's best for me and decline what's unhealthy for me.

- I will be a Queen who will walk in purpose on purpose.

- I will learn from my mistakes.

- I will take care of the Queendom God has blessed me with.

Issuing yourself a royal decree will translate to the people in your life and the ones you encounter. Oh, and best believe, the translation will be effective. You may not even have to utter a single word, but the regality in your spirit will let the people know.

Reigning looks good on you.

The Queen Is Here

By Latoya Garrett

Hear ye, Hear ye

Her Royal Excellence I am she

Make room for this is where I was predestined to be

Long ago, My Creator chose me with a discerning eye

Then enemy with his trickery blinded me to that fact

Years upon years his bait and switch held me in turmoil

Until the glare from my crown piqued my attention

See, I thought my position was the final destination

But God said, "Daughter, you are my heir"

The enemy, scrambling to keep his hold, tried to play the same game

But I said, "No, to the dungeon you shall go"

I'm doing the work now, it's a process

No longer is my head held low but high as the clouds in the sky

My crown stable, my gait light and my spirit wrapped in God's grace and mercy

I know who I am and will forever be

Hear ye, Hear ye

Her Royal Excellence I am she

Make room for this is where I was predestined to be

30-Day Confidence Challenge

You are challenged to pick one thing that scares you, looks daunting, seems unattainable, or difficult. Whatever that "thing" is, you have to do it for the next 30 days. I believe one small change at a time can have the biggest impact on self and the environment around you.

Write you 30-day challenge below.

I _______________________________ am challenging myself to

____

____

for the next 30 days. I can do all things through Christ, and I will conquer this challenge. This is the start of rebuilding my confidence because I deserve to life my best life.

As you go through your challenge, document your progress. Share it with others, and please share it with me (email: confidentqueenpub@gmail.com).

For those who are really stepping forward in confidence, I invite you to allow me to feature your success on social media and YouTube. Email me at the email address above, and I will set up your one-on-one Confident Queen interview.

Let's make this a movement.

CIS Merch

GET YOUR *CONFIDENT IS SHE* SHIRT
https://payhip.com/b/Oq9X4

GET 15% OFF WHEN YOU USE THE CODE: CONFIDENT
NAVY BLUE & WHITE SHIRT OPTIONS (GILDAN 100%)
GOLD LETTERS WILL BE GLITTER HTV

www.ingramcontent.com/pod-product-compliance
Lightning Source LLC
Chambersburg PA
CBHW071338130726
47996CB00002B/788